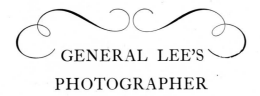

GENERAL LEE'S
PHOTOGRAPHER

GENERAL LEE'S
PHOTOGRAPHER

The Life and Work of Michael Miley

BY

MARSHALL FISHWICK

PUBLISHED FOR

The Virginia Historical Society

by

THE UNIVERSITY OF NORTH CAROLINA PRESS 1954

Gift of R. Bretz
5/9/79

TABLE OF CONTENTS

ACKNOWLEDGMENTS

The Virginia Historical Society, which owns the Miley plates, and which assisted in my research and arranged for publication, made possible the appearance of this volume. The man most responsible was the Society's late director, the Rev. Clayton Torrence. John Jennings and William Rachel have carried on, just as he knew they would.

Many people in Lexington have supplied prints and information, especially Harrington Waddell, Mrs. Finley Waddell, and the late Dr. E. P. Tompkins. Milton Russell and other staff members of the Virginia State Library, which houses the negatives, were always courteous and helpful. So was Paul Vanderbilt at the Library of Congress, who helped with the history of photography, and Frank Scherschel, of *Life* magazine, who made suggestions about the choice of glass plates.

Part of the Introduction appeared in *American Quarterly*, and is used with permission.

MARSHALL W. FISHWICK

Washington and Lee University
Lexington, Virginia

GENERAL LEE'S
PHOTOGRAPHER

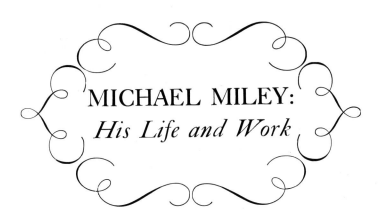

MICHAEL MILEY:
His Life and Work

FOR MANY Southerners and many aspects of Southern society, the Reconstruction era was, in Lanier's poignant words, not so much a matter of living as of not dying. Returning to former homes that were now only blackened chimneys, and to a once proud and thriving section that was now humbled and desolate, the Confederate soldiers had a tremendous job of rehabilitation ahead of them. The presence of an army of occupation, division into military districts, and the use of power by a vindictive opposition party aggravated affairs. As a final blow, Southerners were subjected to statements such as this one, made in 1870 by President Hill of Harvard: "The task for the North is to spread knowledge and culture over the regions that sit in darkness."

The heroic efforts of such Southerners as William Gilmore Simms, Margaret Junkin Preston, John Esten Cooke, Paul Hamilton Hayne, Sidney Lanier, and Henry Timrod to revive Southern arts and letters, despite vast difficulties, have been acknowledged. In a quatrain Timrod expressed the South's determination to build a new culture out of the ruins of the old:

Take with thee all thy gloom
And guilt, and all our griefs, save
what the breast
Without a wrong to some dear
shadowy guest
May not surrender even to the tomb.

This book is about a Southerner of the Reconstruction period whose work has been almost completely ignored to date. His name was Michael Miley, and his field was photography. The record of his life and of his work indicates that he deserves a distinctive place for both his scientific contributions and his aesthetic achieve-

I

ments in this field. Miley spent his life in the small town of Lexington, Virginia. Yet isolation did not tarnish his skill, nor prohibit him from exercising it with his primitive photographic equipment. Only his Lee portraits have been widely viewed up to now; but the prints that follow indicate that his talents extended in many other directions than that of a portrait artist. It is time that Michael Miley's story be told.

Less than a year after General Robert E. Lee had ridden to the same town to take up his duties as president of war-torn Washington College, a young ex-Confederate soldier named Michael Miley entered Lexington, Virginia. He came to open a photographic studio.

There was no show of affection for the shy young man, such as that which citizens had tendered the idolized Lee.[1] Miley had not announced his business plans; he had no relatives in Lexington; he had shown none of the genius that would make him a pioneer photographer of his age. Nothing about his appearance or background would have caused Lexingtonians to single him out for special attention. Small in stature, Miley stood five feet seven inches and weighed one hundred and fifty pounds. His hair was dark

and his keen brown eyes suggested innate intelligence. There was a quiet intensity about him that many friends later commented upon. From the beginning Michael Miley had a reputation for staying clear of matters that did not concern him, of concentrating on his work, and of living within himself.

To understand the careers of either of the newcomers, Lee and Miley, one has to know a few facts about the small county seat to which they came at the end of the Civil War. The 616 square miles that is Rockbridge County is in the west central portion of Virginia, at the southern end of the Shenandoah Valley. Originally part of a grant made to Benjamin Borden in 1737, the town of Lexington was laid off in 1778 as the county seat of Rockbridge County. A fire in 1796 had destroyed the little settlement, and the state legislature had authorized a lottery for raising money to rebuild the destroyed residences.[2] Aided by the presence of Washington College and the Virginia Military Institute, Lexington had prospered during the first half of the nineteenth century. But with the coming of the Civil War, the economy and stability of the county collapsed. Most of the wealth and manpower available were thrown into the cause of the Confeder-

1. When Lee arrived in Lexington on September 18, 1865, after a journey of 108 miles on Traveller, former soldiers gathered about him; Professor James White extended the hospitality of his home; and the college trustees, meeting two days later, discussed "a number of measures for his comfort." See Douglas Southall Freeman, *R. E. Lee* (New York, 1934-35), IV, 227 f.

2. See Edmund P. Tompkins, *Rockbridge County, Virginia: An Informal History* (Richmond, 1952), Chapter II.

acy, and local conditions became desperate. By 1862, citizens were drinking "Confederate coffee" (half wheat and half coffee) and paying thirty dollars a gallon for sorghum. Margaret Junkin Preston, whose diary of the Lexington war years reveals the heroism and suffering of the people, wrote in 1864, "It is astonishing how coolly we talk about the possibility of having to relinquish the Valley, and how our plans take in the probability."

As a corridor for invasion by either army, the valley was of critical importance throughout the Civil War. The northern end was the scene of some of the fiercest and most brilliant fighting by both sides. The region was additionally important as the breadbasket of Virginia. When the destruction of Confederate resources became a primary objective of the Northern Armies, a systematic devastation of the valley was undertaken. In 1864 General David Hunter raided Rockbridge County, destroyed grain and stock and most of the iron furnaces that had flourished there, and bombarded Lexington. By the end of the war the whole area had become an illustration of General Sheridan's remark that even a crow would have to carry rations if it were to attempt to fly across.

It was a poor, ravaged, but proud town to which Michael Miley came in 1866. Money was scarce; even General Lee would get a salary of only $1,500 a year as President of the College. Miley could not expect any extensive patronage, although he might hope to get photographic work from the colleges when they were back in operation. Miley had absolutely no equipment, and there was no other full-time photographer in the county in 1866; he would have to figure out all his problems and policies himself, without outside help. Even if he were able to make a living, he must not expect any great success or recognition for his craftsmanship. Rockbridge County was largely rural, and very few of the farmers would have the money or inclination to sit in his studio.

Yet, with all its economic handicaps, Lexington was an attractive town. Nestled between the Blue Ridge and the Alleghanies, it had a rugged natural charm that no one, especially Michael Miley, could miss. From its hardships and defeat it had acquired a tradition. As a Confederate soldier and a Virginian, Miley was returning to his people. If there was little money around, prices reflected it, and one did not need a large income to live. Most of all, Lexington had in it people, and around it countryside, that Miley wanted to preserve in photographs. He came to Lexington because he saw a chance to do a job which was worth doing, and which he felt he was able to do.

Of Pennsylvania Dutch descent, Michael Miley was born on July 19, 1841, on a Rockingham County farm in the Shenandoah Valley, not many miles

3

north of his eventual home in Lexington. While he was still a boy, his father, Henry Miley,[3] bought a farm farther south on the Great Path which buffalo, Indian, and settler had used as a main artery to the south and west. This farm was three miles from Fairfield on the Brownsburg Road in Rockbridge County; it was Michael Miley's home until he enlisted at the outbreak of the Civil War. Like many farm boys in the 1840's, Miley had little formal education, picking up what "book learning" he could at the hearth and the old field school. His absorption with nature, landscapes, and local history commenced in his boyhood. Michael always spoke of these years in the country as happy ones, and was proud of his ability to make things grow in his Lexington greenhouse. This feeling for the mystery, the wonder, and the symmetry in nature he managed to capture in some of his best photographs.

Hardly twenty when he enlisted, Miley served his native state in the Confederate infantry. His first two years were spent in the famous Stonewall Brigade under General Thomas J. Jackson, whom he admired intensely. The young private always regretted that Stonewall Jackson was killed before he could photograph him. Later on he carefully copied Jackson portraits, and photographed school children and cadets in mourning at the General's grave. As a soldier Miley amused himself by sketching the countryside and the terrain. Even on the field of battle, mountains, trees, and clouds interested him more than military calculations. But his career as both war sketcher and soldier ended for him, as for General Jackson, at Chancellorsville. The day Jackson was shot Miley was captured, hurried to the rear, and marched to the Potomac. There he and other captured Confederates were put aboard the steamship *Spaulding*, which sailed down the river, out into the Atlantic, and up the Delaware Bay, where the prisoners were put ashore on the island known as Fort Delaware. Here he was confined until after Lee's surrender, subjected to a much more harrowing experience than that which he had faced on the front line.

Because a fellow Lexington soldier, James L. McCown, who was captured with Miley (and who later worked for him) kept a detailed diary, we are able to reconstruct many aspects of the prison life in what McCown called "this northern Bastille."[4] Officers and men were separated in the camp, and strict disciplinary measures enforced. Rations were

3. No record remains of Miley's father, whose half-brother was a Presbyterian minister. Michael had two brothers, John and William. His only half-sister, Margaret, married James Burgess and went west.

4. This diary was in the possession of McCown's son, the late Dr. Albert McCown, of Richmond, Virginia. Excerpts from it were published in the *Rockbridge County News* for January 29, 1953.

4

scant (breakfast often consisted of soggy crackers and a cup of coffee) and the climate was bad, so that many of the prisoners succumbed. Every morning a guard duty unit brought in the pine coffins for those who had died during the night. Under the effects of an intestinal disease, poor food, and various other hardships, Miley wasted away to what he called "almost nothing," and barely escaped death in the winter of 1864. A Union doctor, he later recalled, said he would never live to see Virginia again. Yet he managed to pull through, due in part to the care administered by other Rockbridge County men on the island, such as McCown, John Varner, Clay Palmer, C. J. Gillock, and James Bumpass. One of the items the men missed most was tobacco. "There is much suffering for the weed," McCown recorded in his diary.

Among the occasional visitors was Dr. George Junkin, who had been president of Washington College from 1848 to 1860, but who fled to the North when Virginia seceded. He came to the prison to distribute tracts and preach to the ragged rebels. He carried with him a cane which was a present from his son-in-law, Stonewall Jackson!

But for a warning from a Yankee boatman, Miley might never have got home, even after Appomattox and his release. As he was being ferried back to the mainland, he saw a slab of raw bacon on the deck, which he started to eat. "I wouldn't do that if I were you, Reb," said the boatman. "The last man who ate on that bacon died." As Miley threw the contaminated bacon overboard he might have wondered why fate had spared him at this dark hour of his life.

II

Like many a Confederate veteran, he had no job awaiting him. What prompted him to go into photography we do not know. He had artistic leanings (evidenced by his sketching), and the war had shaken him loose from old associations. Photography had at least the possibility of providing a livelihood—which was not true of painting. He might also have been stirred by the work of Matthew Brady or other war photographers.[5] Pos-

---

5. The existence of several Brady photographs (including two of Lee which Brady made in Richmond after the surrender) in Miley's files proves conclusively that Miley was familiar with Brady's work; but we have no way of knowing just how early he came in contact with it. Brady fared no better than Miley during the Brown Decades, so far as finances were concerned. Brady's expenses were so great that he sank ever deeper into debt and lost control of his invaluable Civil War negatives. Three quarters of them were purchased by the War Department at auction for non-payment of storage; others were seized by the photographic supply house of Anthony and Co. in default of payment. Miley died a poor man, but at least the collection of negatives to which he devoted fifty years of his life was passed on to his son.

sibly he felt that in the medium of the camera he could express many of those ideas which he innately felt. In any event he went to Staunton, Virginia, one of the large and important urban centers in the valley, to study with an early Virginia photographer, John Burdette. From him Miley learned the basic elements of photography, and the wet plate method which was then in vogue.[6] Burdette suggested that Miley go into business with him in Staunton, but a powerful personality drew the young novice forty miles south to the smaller town of Lexington: Robert E. Lee.

Miley had no personal contact with General Lee during the war years. Like many another young Southerner, he came to think of Lee as the epitome of the cause for which he was fighting. When he heard that General Lee was coming to Lexington, he decided to document the man and environment for posterity. Even before establishing his studio, he set out to get a photograph of General Lee. He was able to interest a transient photographer named Andrew H. Plecker (later of Lynchburg, Virginia) in the task. Plecker visited Lexington in November, 1866, with his "traveling ferro-type gallery." With him Michael Miley drove the lumbering van to Rockbridge Baths, a few miles north of Lexington, and took the first pictures made of General Lee after he came to the county. Plecker stayed in Lexington for several weeks more, as this advertisement in the November 28, 1866, issue of the Lexington *Gazette and Banner* indicates:

Gallery on wheels, Ladies recollect
I may be off ere you expect.
Pictures good and prices low
Now's your chance before I go!

One can only hope Andrew H. Plecker was a better photographer than he was poet. He moved on according to schedule, and left Michael Miley without a van or studio in which to continue his work. During his stay, Plecker came to respect the judgment of his quiet apprentice. "Miley, I'd rather fight the devil than buck you!" he publicly admitted on one occasion.

Miley's prospects were considerably brightened by meeting again James L. McCown, with whom he had been in prison at Fort Delaware. McCown was unemployed, and he joined Miley as a photographic printer. Someone would

---

6. In the wet plate method, which was the standard process until 1880, each picture represented hours of laborious preparation. Since exposures sometimes required many minutes, the subject's head was held firmly in a vise-like rack, lest the slightest movement nullify a whole day's labor. The photographer had to sensitize, expose, and develop the plate while it was wet; he could not carry it away, but had to develop it on the spot. This necessitated carrying one's dark room with him. The most famous traveling dark room of this epoch was Matthew Brady's "Whatsit," as the Union soldiers called his mule-pulled, tarpaulin-covered contraption. For a description of the wet plate method in the field, see Roy Meredith's *Mr. Lincoln's Camera Man* (New York, 1946).

have to finance them; with McCown's assistance Miley persuaded John C. Boude, a former Confederate captain and wartime friend, to supply the capital. Miley's life had crossed Boude's before, in an experience that neither of them could have remembered pleasantly. Miley had held Boude on the operating table while his leg was amputated in 1862 after he had been wounded in a bloody battle in the valley. One of the first acts of Boude and Miley in November, 1866, was to rent a studio in the Hopkins Building on Main Street. Although badly damaged by war, Lexington was beginning to get on its feet again. The wagons were once more rolling along the Great Path, bring-

ing business to the town. Students were coming from all over the South to study at "General Lee's school." Still, young Miley was not very prosperous on his first Yuletide in Lexington. In fact, he did not have a single penny until somebody dropped in to have a picture taken just before closing on Christmas Eve. On his share of the resulting two dollar fee Michael Miley had to make his holiday.[7] With the new year business improved, and the one employee, James McCown, was paid regularly after January, 1867. An advertisement of Miley's new studio appeared on the January 2, 1867, issue of the Lexington *Gazette and Banner*, and read:

PHOTOGRAPHIC GALLERY
Main Street opposite Presbyterian Church
Lexington, Va.
BOUDE AND MILEY

Having fitted up their Rooms with all the modern improvements are
prepared to take PICTURES
In every style of the art now in use.
Being permanently located here they will spare no pains to make this
GALLERY equal in any respect to city gallerys.
Particular attention paid to copying and enlarging pictures. We will also
color in Oil, India Ink or Water Colors.
 Terms Moderate. Call and see our specimens, whether you
 want pictures or not.
Ladies will find a PIANO in the Reception Room.

One can easily imagine with what excitement and anticipation the young

photographer invited Robert E. Lee to come for a sitting in the studio. Lee not

7. This anecdote appears in a typescript made in 1940 by Michael Miley's son, Henry M. Miley. Now in the archives of the McCormick Library, Washington and Lee University, it contains much valuable material on Michael Miley, the author's father, and reminiscences of the family. It is hereafter referred to as the Henry Miley typescript.

only came once; he came often. He seemed impressed with the shy, sincere, competent young man of twenty-six whom he found waiting for him there. Although Lee disliked having any public recognition, he was very kind to Miley and considered him a friend. The general encouraged him to take photographs of other members of the Lee family, and brought to Miley's studio such well-known guests as Jefferson Davis, General P. G. T. Beauregard, General Jubal A. Early, and General John C. Breckinridge. As a result of Lee's cooperation, the historical value of Miley's collection was greatly enhanced. Summarizing Miley's opinion of Lee, his son Henry Miley said: "My father never saw a man more willing to oblige than General Lee. Lee would tell him just to take his time, because he and his guest had plenty of time and nothing to do. Father said he was very different from other men, who would come in with people visiting them and be impatient. He considered Lee the greatest man that ever lived." [8]

During his own sittings, Lee talked to his new-found photographer friend about his early childhood, and of his interest in the scenery about Lexington; but he never mentioned the war. He had, Miley observed, the largest head of any man he ever photographed.

Of all the Lee photographs Miley made, the most popular, although not in Miley's opinion the best, was the 1868 portrait of Lee on Traveller. This picture was made at the General's request. He told Michael Miley one morning to photograph him in uniform, mounted on Traveller, "just as we went through the four years of war together." This was the first and only time he requested his picture taken in a Confederate uniform. Miley completed the necessary arrangements. The photograph was made the following afternoon in the garden behind the Lee home, on the Washington College campus. It was a warm day and the flies bothered Traveller. Several negatives were spoiled by his flicking tail before a successful plate was made.

Miley was on hand to record the final rites when in 1870 the leading hero of the South was laid to rest. One photograph shows the casket with two students on guard. Another shows the crowd of mourners and the assembly about the chapel, with the buildings and the columns of the college draped in black crepe; still another shows the funeral procession as it passed down Main Street. Shortly after the funeral, Miley photographed the General's office just as Lee left it for the last time. These photographs are among the most moving of all Miley made. They are not only historical documents, but a personal commentary upon the death of a dear friend.

An intimate association developed be-

8. Henry Miley typescript, p. 7.

tween Miley and the sculptor Edward V. Valentine (1838-1930), during Reconstruction days. Mr. Valentine first came to Lexington in May, 1870, to begin work on a bust of General Lee from life. In June he had Miley make several photographs of Lee from different angles in order to facilitate the sculpturing and eliminate the necessity of long tiresome sittings. After the bust was finished, the artist could find no one to take a satisfactory photograph of it; so Miley went to Richmond at the sculptor's request and took one which pleased Valentine immensely. The friendship was renewed when Valentine began work on the statue of Stonewall Jackson which stands today at Jackson's tomb in the Lexington Presbyterian Cemetery. Later on Miley took a number of pictures of Valentine's recumbent statue of Lee, both before and after it was placed in Lee Chapel. He sold hundreds of these prints, thus helping to link the name of Valentine closely with that of Lee.

Business had so prospered with the rejuvenation of Washington College and V.M.I. that by 1870 Miley was able to buy out Boude's interest and continue as his own master. In this spring he married Martha T. Mackey, seven years his junior, who lived a few miles outside Lexington near Riverside on the South River.[9] Their honeymoon was a trip to Philadelphia, where Miley enjoyed having their pictures made by another photographer. After Miley and his bride returned to Lexington, they lived in the McLaughlin house on Lee Avenue and Washington Street. The next spring they occupied an apartment in the Hopkins Building, directly across the hall from Miley's studio. Here two sons were born, Herbert in 1871 and Henry Mackey in 1873. Eight months after Henry's birth, Miley bought a two-story white frame house in the fashionable west side of town. Here he lived peacefully until his death in 1918. Few if any of his neighbors realized that his work was of special significance, most of them considering him as an introvert. Unlike such artistic contemporaries as Herman Melville, Emily Dickinson, and Albert Ryder, Miley did not become embittered by his modest circumstances. He was much more closely allied to the medieval artist-guildsman than to the nineteenth-century romantic poet. By his own efforts and industry he was able to make an adequate income in a small Southern town; certainly he was the only man in Lexington who could be said to thrive off his art. He enjoyed the locality and the college contacts, and received enough outside recognition to realize that his talents were not totally unappreciated. Dedicated to his work, which he practiced in and out

9. Mrs. Robert E. Lee, while still in mourning after her husband's death, wrote a cordial letter of congratulation to the newlyweds; later on she knitted a little cape for Herbert, their first son.

of professional hours, and devoted to his wife, whose illness made it difficult for her to travel, he found a good life in Lexington, and had little impulse to change it.

III

To his Lexington neighbors, who did not know what technical and aesthetic problems Miley had tackled, his life seemed quite normal, perhaps even a little pedestrian. He was fond of his home, and in 1886 had it renovated and weatherboarded. Gardening was his favorite avocation, and he was proud of having the first spring flowers or vegetables in the area. He developed a knack for grafting, and succeeded in producing four different varieties of apples on one of his trees. To better his garden facilities, he built a greenhouse on the southeast side of his home and raised rare plants. Palms and century plants grew in his front yard during summer months. Although he had a man to help him, Miley planted everything himself, to be certain it was done just as he wanted it. Often he arose early in the morning to "get out and see things grow." He sat up many a night in bitter cold weather tending fires in the greenhouse to keep his plants from freezing, using nearly as much coal in the process as was needed to keep the main house comfortable. There were no florists in Lexington at this time, and the Mileys were most generous in giving flowers to neighbors and to the sick people of the town. This closeness to nature not only affected his home life, but also his photographs. Frequently Miley would leave his studio and dash off to take an outdoor picture if he thought a special cloud arrangement, sunset, or circumstance warranted it. His son recalled: "Father was always looking for special cloud effects. He would have the carriage ready in case he saw a chance arrangement worth getting, and would rush down to the bend in North River before the cloud left. Sometimes he would take plates as large as 24" by 24" with an immense camera, so as to get the best effect. Nature was to him an endless boundless fascination."

Miley's freedom to range far from home, and to spend a full day at his work, was sharply curtailed in 1876 when Mrs. Miley became a semi-invalid. For years she was never able to walk more than a short distance at a time. Henry recalled in later life that he had never heard his mother utter a sharp word to anyone; nor could he remember ever having seen her leave the neighborhood alone. She was meticulous and neat in her dress. Her main ambition in life was to make her home attractive and comfortable for her husband and sons. Michael usually accompanied his wife on her afternoon ride in the carriage. His devotion to his family and routine was a central feature of Miley's life.

The second son, Henry Mackey Miley,

exhibited deep interest in the photographic process. As a youngster, he was employed by his father to retouch glass plates, getting five cents for an 8x10 portrait and a dime for larger plates. One negative would often consume all of the boy's energies for an entire day; but like his father, he enjoyed the work and took pride in his results. Henry Miley entered Washington and Lee University in September, 1890. His courses were those of most college students of his day: Latin, German, English, all the mathematics offered, history, moral philosophy, geology, biology, and chemistry. His closest faculty friendship was with Dr. William G. Brown, chemistry professor, who gave Henry much encouragement and assistance. Later on, Henry's grasp of the scientific method and acquaintance with chemistry was helpful in the photographic experiments conducted at the Miley studios. He received his A.B. degree in June, 1894, and went to work as a full-time assistant to his father. The next year the name was changed from Miley's Carbon Studio to M. Miley and Son, and contracts for the two school annuals (*Calyx* of Washington and Lee, and *The Bomb* of V.M.I.) obtained. This was the first year of regular publication for both institutions.[10] As the thousands of student portraits in the Miley Collection make clear, it was this college work

that provided the family with the bulk of their revenue.

Though he had little formal education, Michael Miley had a scientific turn of mind and an insatiable curiosity in regard to things about him. The range of his reading was not great, but he read serious books and retained the information they imparted. His chemical knowledge was gained largely from his own experience, and he acquired a familiarity with most chemical reactions which pertained to photography. If his equipment and interests were relatively limited, Michael Miley nevertheless exemplified the best traditions and methods of scientific research.

During the first half of Miley's career three great scientific advances revolutionized the field of photography. First and most important, the gelatine-bromide dry plate process was perfected, which eliminated the overwhelming handicaps of the wet plate, and led eventually to instantaneous work and the hand camera. The introduction of ortho-chromatic emulsions, guaranteeing the success of color photography and reproduction, was the second. The perfection of first the "hot bath" and then the "cold bath" platino-type was the third achievement, giving prints a quality surpassing everything which had preceded them. One of the noteworthy features of the Miley

10. The first issue of *The Bomb* appeared in 1885, but it was ten years before a second one appeared. The 1895 *Calyx* was the first issued, although Washington and Lee had had a literary magazine, *The Southern Collegian*, since 1868.

I I

story is the rapidity with which, despite his isolation, he discovered and utilized these and other improvements.

Occasionally Miley left the county, as in 1876, when he visited the Philadelphia Centennial Exhibition. While engaged in experiments of his own, he sometimes went to New York to converse with other photographers. This revealing account of his visit to the studio of a fashionable New York photographer named Sarony has been preserved by Henry Miley: "When father visited Sarony's he talked with all the employees, who said he had a lot of nerve for a country boy. They were uppish with him because they knew he was from a little town down South. Just to be smart, they asked father how he was getting along. They were surprised to learn he was not only using dry plates, but making his own. After that they crowded around, asking for the formula. He gave it to them."

When after 1876 the first gelatine-bromide or dry plate equipment proved to be quite expensive, Miley started coating his own plates.[11] In addition to his own experiments, he relied on articles in *Wilson's Photographic Magazine*, a lead-ing photographic journal of the day, which he read with interest.[12] To prepare his bromide and silver emulsions, he boiled them over a small stove in his laboratory, later putting the film over his own glass. Even after commercial plates became cheaper, he still preferred to make his own. This individualistic streak in Miley was one of his chief assets.

While experimenting with home-made dry plates in the early 1880's, Miley made an important discovery which has since been adopted by film manufacturers. To appreciate its nature, one must under-stand a problem of nineteenth-century photography known as halation. Hala-tion is a phenomenon which causes a halo-like effect in certain areas of a picture when light reaching the plate penetrates the film and is reflected back by the rear surface of the plate. It was a source of great irritation to practicing photographers. While Miley was experi-menting with his own emulsions, he noticed that during the boiling process the emulsion was yellowish in color and not very sensitive. As it cooked further, it turned blue and became much faster. Miley reasoned that if the yellow emul-

11. The most comprehensive history of these photographic advances, despite its chauvinism, is Josef M. Eder's *History of Photography*, Edward Epstean translation (New York, 1945). Robert Taft's *Photography and the American Scene* (New York, 1938), relates photographic matters to social his-tory, and Beaumont Newhall's *Photography, 1839-1937* (New York, 1937), brings together a number of classic photographs of this country and Europe. Newhall's book also contains (p. 91 f.) a good bib-liography of books in this field.

12. Begun in 1864, with Edward L. Wilson as editor, the journal continued until 1888 as the *Philadelphia Photographer*. From 1889 until 1914 it was called *Wilson's Photographic Magazine*, at which time it was merged with *Camera*.

sion were slow and the blue fast, by coating his plates first with the slow emulsion and then with the fast, the fast emulsion could be exposed and the exposure terminated before the light would have time to pass through the slow emulsion and reflect back.

The results were extremely satisfactory and Miley was apparently the first user of non-halation plates in this country. Dr. William G. Brown of the Washington and Lee University Department of Chemistry became so enthusiastic over this new process that he wanted to join Miley in starting a plant to manufacture the plates. For some unknown reason, the plan never went into effect. On a trip to New York, Miley passed on his findings to photographers there. Within a few years the first commercial non-halation plates appeared on the market, produced north of the Potomac.

The generous and unprotective way in which Miley revealed his discoveries and methods explains why he did not benefit financially from them or receive historical credit for his work. Just which photographers or inventors actually pirated his findings, unintentionally or by design, and why he did not exercise more caution in talking about his work, we shall never know. There can be no question of his ingenuity. He was concerned with what he could do, and not with what he could acquire. Miley represents one of the finest types that American civilization has produced.

IV

Miley made some of his best prints by what is known as the carbon transfer process. A technique used for ordinary printing, it gave him his start in color work. Instead of projecting three images by lights of the three primary colors, Miley changed each positive image into a dye image, the color being complementary to that of the filter by which its corresponding negative was made. Such work was tedious and demanding, and was undertaken for experimental reasons rather than financial gain. Michael Miley was proud of his early carbon transfers, and hung the best of them on his studio wall. Pictures of local belles such as Frances Howe, Gertrude Jacceri, Margaret Graham, and Minnie Kate Varner reflected his chivalrous notion of womanhood, long a trait of the Southern mind. Miley's extensive experience gained in experimenting with carbon transfers suggested the possibility of natural color photography, and laid the foundation for his most notable contribution to photographic science.

Interest in recording colored images goes back at least to Isaac Newton's famous 1672 paper on the corpuscular nature of light, presented to the Royal Society. The work of Huygens, Young, Seebeck, and Herschel kept this interest alive, but it is Louis Ducos du Hauron

13

who must be called the father of color photography. He presented to the Paris Photographic Society on May 7, 1869, the first recognizable, successful three-color photograph ever made. His method was to employ three films of collodion, each covered with a film of dichromated gelatin, red, yellow, and blue, respectively. On December 18,1885, he took out French patent 173,012 on his process, seventeen years before Miley filed his patent papers in America.[13]

The Lumière brothers, Auguste and Louis, also deserve a high place in the development of color photography. They used red, green, and violet filters on specially sensitized plates, and were finally able to take a colored picture on a single plate. In 1907 Auguste came to the United States with a grandson, and in collaboration with his American representative, Jules Brulatour, began making "Autochrome" film. This was the first color photographic material successfully employed in America. A leading photographic journal heralded the new day: "It seems that the thing that all photographers from Daguerre down have dreamed about has at last come to pass—the reproduction of an object in its natural colors as seen by the eye, by a single exposure with an ordinary camera."[14]

In Berlin, meanwhile, Professor Herman W. Vogel had been working on color sensitizers which made it possible to arrive at the correct tone values by a scientific formula. Impressed with Vogel's work, the firm of William Kurtz in New York offered to buy his process and adapt it for halftone relief printing. Vogel came to New York in 1892 and completed arrangements. His first azaline plates are now preserved in the American Museum of Photography in Philadelphia. (One of them is reproduced as the frontispiece to Louis Sipley's *A Half Century of Color*.) Kurtz's company failed, despite the fact that he poured $200,000 into experiments. The result was a 1902 merger of the National Colotype Company, the American Three-Color Company, and the Osborne Company of Newark, New Jersey. A few years before, the *Saturday Evening Post* for September 30, 1899, had featured for the first time a three-color cover, barely beating the twentieth century to the punch.

The American who figured most prominently in the first decade of color work was Frederic Eugene Ives of Philadelphia. Using a triple projection lantern and three diapositives (backed by red, green, and violet glass), he projected

13. Of the various books dealing with color photography, the best is Edward J. Wall, *The History of Three-Color Photography* (Boston, 1925). Other important volumes are Carlton E. Dunn, *Natural Color Processes* (Boston, 1938); Joseph S. Friedman, *History of Color Photography* (Boston, 1944), and Louis W. Sipley, *A Half Century of Color* (New York, 1952).

14. *Wilson's Photographic Magazine*, 44 (October, 1907), 610.

three-color pictures. Ives called his portable apparatus, a peep-hole affair through which the three transparencies could be optically united, a "kromskop." The George Eastman House in Rochester, New York, has Ives' original apparatus, and shows his actual photographs regularly. For his work the Franklin Institute commended Ives, as it did Miley a few years later. By 1897 Ives had made his three-color projection serviceable for motion picture photography. T. T. Baker, J. W. Bennetto, and J. Joly were advancing the color photography technique in other parts of the world as the century drew to a close.

How does Miley fit into the picture? It was his early work in carbon transfer that caused him to drift over into color work; but it was work done in comparative isolation, with no correspondence or aid from scientists outside Miley's immediate ken. Except for some aid from his friend William Brown, Professor of Chemistry at Washington and Lee, Miley worked alone. True enough, he might have had access to certain photographic journals. Several copies of *Wilson's Photographic Magazine* were left in his library; and although no copies have been found by his heirs, he might have seen the *British Journal of Photography, The St.* *Louis Practical Photographer,* or *Camera.*[15] No one can doubt, however, that the patents Miley took out in 1902 represented original research which had not been written up in any journal.

Miley's first success with color photography came in 1897, after his family had returned from a vacation at Rockbridge Alum Springs. The father and son were working as a team, but Michael Miley conceived the idea and set up the project. From his previous work Miley knew that he could complement the true primary colors (blue, green, and red) with the subtractive primaries, yellow, magenta, and cyan. If from white you subtract blue, the result is green and red, which mix to make yellow. If from white you subtract green, the result is blue and red, which mix to make magenta. If from white you subtract red, the result is blue and green, which mix to make cyan. By laying down dyes one on the other, and of varying depths, all other colors can be produced.

For his experiments Miley used the standard Wratten tricolor filters, numbers 24, 47, and 58. By skillful masking he overcame their shortcomings in relation to the spectral quality of the printing dyes. He made three successive exposures of his subject through his three filters,

---

15. The *British Journal of Photography* was published from 1864 to 1919. J. H. Fitzgibbon published *The St. Louis Practical Photographer* from 1877 to 1910, after which it became *The St. Louis and Canadian Photographer.* The first issue of *Camera* appeared in Philadelphia in July, 1897. Until 1900 it was "the official organ of the Columbia Photographic Society." Files of all these publications may be found in the Library of Congress.

timing them according to the illumination so as to give three balanced negatives. (Since this could only be done with a still-life subject, he concentrated on bowls of fruit and oil portraits.) To make color prints he had to make three positives from his negatives, using the complementary colors. Edward Wall pays homage to Miley's tireless research in his monumental *History of Three-Color Photography*, and includes this technical description of Miley's process: "Mr. Miley prepared the temporary support first with a solution of wax and resin, then coated with collodion. After drying, the prints were stripped, their surface rubbed with a mixture of equal parts of ether and alcohol (to remove wax and collodion) and then cemented with gelatin and chrome alum solution." [16]

Michael Miley's most important scientific achievement was undoubtedly his early work in color. The history of the development of color photography is an extremely complicated one; and even though we have the evidence of a patent that Miley took out in 1902, it is difficult to evaluate the importance of his contribution or of the extent to which his work affected other pioneers in this field. What cannot be disputed is the fact that, experimenting in isolation and working out his problems in his own way, he was responsible for some of the earliest color photographs ever produced, and some of the best produced during the experimental age of color photography. Unfortunately Michael Miley did not keep full notes of his experiments, and we have no way of telling just what part of his work was ahead of that being done elsewhere. From a study of the sometimes contradictory source material of the history of color photography, one concludes that Miley was not a key figure so far as new principles were concerned. Certainly he was not as important as du Hauron or Lumière in France, or Ives or Kurtz in Philadelphia and New York. Yet Miley did increase the efficiency of color work, and help the whole field to advance. He was one of the lesser experimenters who made it possible for the giants in the field to move ahead rapidly. The wonder is not that he did not do more, but that he did as much as he did.

In 1902 Benjamin Cable, a New York businessman and former chairman of the Democratic party, became interested in Miley, having seen one of his color prints while traveling. With his lawyer, James Bailey, he came to Lexington to interview the man whose color work was so remarkable and life-like. At Cable's insistence and with his financial backing, they secured a patent for their process. Cable wanted to make the Mileys equal partners with himself in a company to produce color photographs. It looked as

16. Wall, *op. cit.*, p. 327.

if Miley's career as an isolated small-town photographer were over. On October 21, 1902, U. S. patent 711,875 was issued to "Michael and Henry Mackey Miley, of Lexington, Virginia, assignors to Miley Colour Photograph Company of New York." [17]

Mr. Cable was anxious to promote the company and sell shares of stock to the public. At this point, Michael Miley resolutely called a halt. He told Cable that because of the difficulty of the process and necessity of personal supervision, he did not believe the color prints could be mass-produced and sold commercially. Emphatically Miley declared: "I do not want anyone to buy stock in a company which will connect the name of Miley with inferior craftsmanship." Vigorously and vainly Cable argued. Promotion of the company was abandoned. Most of the people of Lexington considered Miley foolish for turning down such an excellent opportunity for making a fortune. Miley, with his unbounded personal integrity, preferred to work on in his own way, and by his own standards.

Contrary to the ill will one would have expected from Cable at his disappointment, he retained his enthusiasm for the uncompromising Miley. In 1906 he sent him a valuable J. H. Henner painting, *Saint Fabolia*, to be copied. Miley did so with extraordinary fidelity, fascinated by the young saint clad in a red hood. Still Miley himself was not satisfied. Five or six prints were made, none of which he considered good enough to be sent to Cable.

The early color photographs were of stationary objects, since the exposure time required through the dark filters prohibited using living or moving subjects. Among the paintings successfully reproduced in color by the Mileys were: Peale's portraits of George Washington and Lafayette; Pioto's portrait of Lee; and the Lee family paintings of Daniel Parke Custis and his wife Martha. Michael Miley's untiring experimentation and modifications of formulae are verified by the hundreds of scrawled notations on the back of unsuccessful or damaged proofs. In these minute scribblings can be read the tortuous evolution of the Miley process, and the unending quest of Michael Miley for a more vivid and flexible art form by the use of the new medium of photography. His achievement has been overlooked in the lightning development of various phases of the field. Not that it was widely recognized even in his own day, or town. One of the rare tributes he received came in 1905 when the Franklin Institute of Philadelphia awarded him the Edward Longstreth Medal of Merit for his discoveries.[18] The

---

17. The following foreign patents were also obtained: England, EP 17,485 (1902); Belgium, BelgP. 165,082 (1902); France, FP 324,813; Canada, CanP. 79,192.

18. An abstract of the report is published in the *Journal of the Franklin Institute*, 159 (June, 1905), 470-72.

citation dated May 3, 1905, and signed by President John Birkinbine, relates that the distinctive feature of the Miley process consists in the method of imparting the requisite color to the respective tissues of gelatine, "which he effects by the use of finely ground pigments of red, yellow and blue, achieving a spectroscopic color value equal to, or approximating, the color value of the corresponding primary in the original subject."

V

In 1907 an event occurred that destroyed forever many Miley negatives, and most of Miley's papers, notes, and accounts. Henry Miley wrote about it thus: "On Saturday afternoon, October 12, 1907, I went down to Mrs. A. N. Glasgow's to spend Sunday. Father was at home. My aunt called me to the phone. I was told that Hess' Store, just below the Studio, was on fire. Harry Glasgow rushed me to Lexington in a buggy. When I got to town, the building was about burned up. Everything in the front room was totally destroyed. All the registered negatives from 1894 to 1905 were destroyed, but the older negatives were intact. The back room was not injured by fire, and the instruments were saved. Our negatives were insured only for the value of the glass. The fire was thought to have been caused from a defective chimney in the *Rockbridge County News* office." [19]

What photographic treasures and historic papers went up in smoke that Sunday morning, no one can say. Certainly this untabulated loss has been one of the major factors which has caused Miley to be neglected in the two succeeding generations. Michael Miley, in his mid-sixties, had to salvage what he could from the ashes of his studio, and to move his business down the street into temporary quarters in the Stuart Building. His enthusiasm for color photography and the tedious but superb carbon prints which he had spent years developing were not damaged. In these latter years he made some of his best photographs, continuing to record faithfully the personalities and life of Lexington. He was, in the best sense of the word, a regionalist, enjoying all phases of the life about him, trying to utilize them in his art without being sentimental or chauvinistic.

Although Michael Miley's most original phase was completed by the turn of the century, he worked steadily until his death in 1918. "Father wouldn't give up," Henry Miley reported. "Although he left most of the studio work up to me after 1910, he always gave suggestions

Some of Miley's most successful early color work was done with fruit. He made over fifty trial prints before he got this one of a bowl of peaches (c. 1903)

19. Henry Miley typescript, p. 9.

and criticisms." In his seventy-third year the elder Miley undertook one of his most difficult assignments: photographing in color Clinedinst's monumental painting of "The Battle of New Market" in Jackson Hall at the Virginia Military Institute. He had to construct a special platform in the building fifty feet from the painting and try dozens of exposures before getting results which seemed adequate. The negatives made with the red filter required an exposure of three hours, and those with green and violet filters only slightly less time. Never really satisfied with the results, Miley destroyed most of the negatives he had so laboriously exposed.

Old age did not deprive Michael Miley of good health or innate interest in the world around him. He attended the first motion pictures brought to Lexington, and studied the lighting effects closely; he followed the progress of World War I with the greatest interest, and expressed the hope that he would live to see the final Allied victory. But fate decreed otherwise. Five months before news of the Armistice set Americans dancing in the streets, Michael Miley died in his quiet Lexington home. Since his son was in mourning with the family, there was no photographer to record the funeral rites, as Michael Miley had done those of General Lee a half century earlier. His death was not noted outside Rockbridge County. Few townspeople realized that a great artist had been taken from them. Although the Miley Studio was to re-main open until 1935, Henry Miley contracted tuberculosis and was forced to undergo treatment at a sanitarium. Unable to interest local institutions in the purchase of the Miley negatives, he agreed to sell all of them, along with his equipment, to the Virginia Historical Society in Richmond. The sale was completed on April 16, 1940. Shortly afterwards the two tons of Belgian glass negatives which represented Michael Miley's life work were carried away by truck. No one continued the Miley studio. Only the elder Lexingtonians remember the man who documented life in the Reconstruction period so painstakingly, so methodically, and so well. If you visit the Lexington Presbyterian Cemetery to see his grave, you will find no tablet or monument to honor him, nor even a Miley plot in the Record Office. Instead, in the corner of another family's lot, you will see a small stone inscribed simply: "M. Miley. 1841-1918." Even this brief inscription is obscured by the gray iron Confederate cross that marks every Southern soldier's grave. The Confederate motto, in Miley's case, seems particularly appropriate: *deo vindice.*

VI

This bare account of an outwardly uneventful and inarticulate life does not begin to communicate the true significance of Michael Miley. Only his extensive collection of photographic negatives, one of the Southern historical monuments of the late nineteenth century, does that. Neither words nor the most detailed painting can ever evoke aspects of the region's past so honestly and completely as these thousands of sensitized glass plates. In bequeathing them to us Miley not only documented the American scene, he left behind an enduring record of himself as artist and of his period as history. For Miley had a keen sense of history and of his obligation to record it. He devoted countless hours to the copying of ancient daguerreotypes of pioneers; of early judges and state officials; and of circuit-riding preachers of the gospel who carried religion to the new frontiers. There are negatives of scores of less prominent people, everyday people, who conducted the daily business and set the tone of small-town Virginia; and of the day laborers, Negroes, and village characters who were just as apt to be preserved on a Miley plate as were the great Confederate generals who flocked to Lexington to see their former chieftain.

Convinced that Lee was "the greatest man who ever lived," Miley, the former Confederate soldier, devoted his brilliant professional capacity, between 1866 and 1870, to recording the spiritual aspects and implications of Lee's twilight years. Not only did he turn his lens as frequently as circumstances permitted on Lee himself, but he meticulously copied all of the available Washington, Custis, and Lee family pictures that came within his ken. He photographed the various Lee statues and memorials, homes, office, and personalia; he even reproduced on glass various crucial Lee letters and documents, such as his commission in the U.S. Army, his letter accepting the presidency of Washington College, and his will. Our knowledge of the Lee story is infinitely enriched by Miley's documentation of it. Other personalities and aspects of the Confederacy are also prominent in the Miley files. There is a group of negatives centering around that other great Lexington warrior and Miley's commander in battle, Stonewall Jackson; copies of famous Brady prints, in which Miley was interested; and more than a score of negatives of former Confederate officers and politicians who visited General Lee and obliged him by sitting for Miley.

Literally thousands of negatives record the story and life of two famous Virginia schools, Washington and Lee University and Virginia Military Institute. Miley tried to keep a complete file of former heads of each and of all faculty members. Because he did the yearbooks for both institutions, he naturally had plates of almost all the young men who came to Lexington from 1895 until his death. His son continued to take college portraits until his retirement in 1935. These portraits, plus those of faculty members, visitors, and townspeople, constitute the great bulk of the Miley Collection and explain why so many portraits have been included in this selection of his work.[20]

Although not so large in number, the remaining landscapes and nature studies are of greater interest to the public at large. Unfortunately, these glass negatives have not yet been catalogued or arranged. Miley was interested not only in people and group scenes, but in history, architecture, and the tempo of life around him. These are the pictures he made for his own amusement and for posterity. He has caught the early Greek Revival manor house in a state of decay; the early automobile bogged down in mud; the old stone ruins of Liberty Hall basking in spring sunlight. Sensing that Southern values were changing rapidly, he worked steadily on little-used roads, in quiet fields, and outside country stores, documenting the life of rural nineteenth-century America before industrialization took command. He earned his living and fed his family by taking family portraits and college class pictures. He earned his freedom and fed his soul by moving out into the county with his camera to record what he saw and what he devised in his mind's eye. His essential greatness rests on the studies he made after the chore work was done.

When we have discussed these portions of the Miley collection, we have yet to mention the one which best displays his aesthetic greatness: his nature pictures. Miley was a lifelong student of all phases of nature, but particularly of the Blue Ridge and Alleghany Mountains which he once described as "the central feature of our whole life." He felt their overwhelming power, their subtlety, their timelessness. He captured on glass some of the mountains' brooding majesty.

The Miley landscapes, full of memory and spirituality, have a definite emotional suggestion; they are creations, much in the way that the landscape that emerges under the painter's brush is a creation. For like the important painters, Miley always attempted to generalize his scenes, making an abstract of form, light, color, and atmosphere, yet not obscuring the characteristic features. He was able to give sufficient details to stir the imagination, yet not detract from the total pattern before him. He entered into nature with an enthusiasm and understanding that made him at home there. Becoming imbued with serenity and insight, he dwelt unerringly on the large and profound qualities of landscape. Because he felt so deeply the inner meaning of the world around him, he contrived to communicate this meaning to us through glass plates.

In viewing Miley's landscapes one can

20. In a letter dated October 17, 1941, T. C. Carrington states that he had intended to classify and identify all the college negatives. But he had just been given a job with the Virginia Defense Council, which would make it necessary for him to abandon the Miley negatives. No professional sorting or preserving has been done since then. A fuller sketch of Carrington appears in the Appendix.

see that his ideas and techniques show much similarity to those of a later and more famous photographer, Alfred Stieglitz. Miley never joined any national photographic groups, and was an old man when Stieglitz's "Society of Amateur Photographers" and "Camera Club" came into their own. Yet Stieglitz's famous pronouncement about Lake George, New York, sums up what Miley might have said about Lexington, Virginia: "I wanted to photograph clouds to find out what I had learned in 40 years about photography. Through clouds to put down my philosophy of life—to show that my photographs were not due to subject matter—nor to special trees, or faces, or interiors, to special privileges. Clouds were there for everyone—no tax on them yet—free."[21]

One of Miley's finest pictures is of clouds and bears the title "Volcano Erupting over House Mountain." In 1874 he looked out his studio window and saw a cloud arrangement that made House Mountain, which watches over Lexington like a mother hen over her chicks, appear to be erupting instead of resting in silent splendor. Miley dashed out to his darkroom-on-wheels, drove the horse wildly down Main Street to the North River, and there took a wet-plate photograph as the sun disappeared behind the mountain. It is included among the prints that follow. Stieglitz, or anyone for that matter, would have been proud of it.

Miley's camera was no mere machine but a delicate instrument, sensitive to things which he felt but never expressed verbally. His understanding of composition was such that he could instinctively distinguish the varying effect of light upon different objects out-of-doors.[22] Without studied effort he made the most of the fact that the greater diffusion of light out of doors tends to flatten objects, reducing the appearance of bulk which they assume in the partial light of the studio. In his best landscapes, Miley combined the two main streams of photography, the utilitarian and the aesthetic, with remarkable success. He infused these pictures with an individuality so that they revealed not only a natural beauty, but also his own personal conceptions of matter as well. His background as a boy on a farm, as a soldier marching up and down the Shenandoah Valley, and as a citizen who loved to slip away from Lexington and rove through the foothills of Rockbridge County, all worked their way into his photographs. This concern

21. Stieglitz's letter to *The Amateur Photographer*, Sept. 19, 1923. Quoted by Beaumont Newhall, *op. cit.*, p. 64.

22. No completely adequate work on the aesthetics of photography exists. One can acquire much valuable information from Charles H. Caffin, *Photography as a Fine Art* (New York, 1901); L. Moholy-Nagy, *Malerei, Photographie, Film* (Munich, 1925); Werner Graff's *Es Kommt der Neue Fotograf!* (Berlin, 1929); Waldo Frank, *America and Alfred Stieglitz* (New York, 1934); and O. W. Larkin, *Art and Life in America* (New York, 1949).

with nature, plus his equally deep interest in science, made Miley a fine craftsman, and occasionally a superb artist as well. Year after year he worked in and out of his studio, expressing himself in the medium he had slowly but thoroughly come to master.

Here is a man, self-disciplined, educated into his métier by an innate sense of proportion and taste, standing four-square against that which was shoddy and ephemeral in his age.

Many questions concerning Michael Miley remain unanswered. As the few people who knew him pass on, the chance of their ever being fully answered dwindles. Yet we know enough about him to perceive that his was a talent to be reckoned with. He worked well enough to be remembered. He refused to exploit his important discoveries, because he thought mass production would lead to an inferior product. Miley's scientific knowledge served as a complement to his aesthetic conscience, much as a working knowledge of anatomy aids a painter who would convey the poetry of the human form.

Not for profit or acclaim, but for inner satisfaction, did Miley work; hence only he could decide how successful his life really was. So far as an outsider can tell, he had ample reason to be satisfied. Virginia, so absorbed with political and social matters that it glances infrequently into the realm of art, can be proud of Michael Miley. So can America. As long as his negatives and prints are in existence, we shall always know what his portion of the world was like, and why, in a century of disillusionment and doubt, we have a culture worth preserving. This is the land; we have our inheritance.

The R. E. Lee Memorial Episcopal Church was finished in 1883, and was photographed often by Miley in the years following. (c. 1905)

LEE GROUP

This portrait of Lee on Traveller, made in 1868, was the most popular Miley ever took. It may still be found hung on parlor walls and circulated on post cards throughout the South. (11 x 11. 1868)

In January 1870 Lee sat before Miley's lens for the last time. This simple, almost classical, picture was the result. (5 x 8. 1870)

Mary Ann Randolph Custis Lee, the General's devoted wife and mother of his seven children, smiled for Miley, despite the discomfort of arthritis, which made her an invalid for years. (4 x 5. c. 1874)

Mary (left) was the oldest and Mildred (right) the youngest of the four daughters, none of whom married. (each 4 x 5. c. 1870)

Among the many daguerreotypes Miley copied was this one of Mrs. George Washington Parke Custis (1788-1852), granddaughter of Martha Washington and mother of Mrs. Robert E. Lee. (5 x 7. An 1866 copy)

These are the sons of Robert E. Lee. Left to right, Robert Edward (1843-1914), George Washington Custis (1832-1913), and William H. Fitzhugh (1837-1891). (5 x 8. c. 1885)

The top graduate in the 1854 class at West Point, George Washington Custis Lee posed proudly for his graduation picture. He succeeded his father as president of Washington and Lee University. (4 x 6. An 1867 copy)

This daguerreotype, which General Lee's daughter Agnes brought to Miley to be copied, is believed to be a picture of her father made in New York in 1845. He would have been 38, and the boy, "Rooney," eight. Miley placed two prints together for use in the pride of the nineteenth-century parlor, the stereoscope. (3 x 4. An 1866 copy)

This is how Lee's office looked the day he died. It has not been changed since.

(8 x 10. 1870)

This 1868 portrait of Lee accentuates his leonine head and small feet. It was made beside Miley's favorite studio table.

(6 x 9. 1868)

31

By the late 1860's the tremendous strain
and worry of the war years became very
marked in the General's face. (8 x 10. 1869)

The Lee Chapel in Lexington is called "the Shrine of the South." The sculptor Edward V. Valentine chose as the theme for the central statue Lee asleep on the field of battle. (above, 11 x 14, 1890; below, 11 x 22, 1883)

The school's Greek columns were draped in black
for Lee's funeral. The uniformed figures are cadets
from the Virginia Military Institute. (11 x 14. 1870)

Everyone who could came to hear the funeral orations lauding Lee. (11 x 14. 1870)

People gathered hours before the actual ceremonies. It was a day they would tell their grandchildren about. (11 x 14. 1870)

36

As Lee's funeral procession turned on to Main Street, Miley's historic instinct overcame his grief; he stuck his camera out of the studio window and made this picture. (11 x 14. 1870)

WILLIAM WHITE AND SONS

For years afterwards visitors stopped where General Lee had first stayed in Lexington—the National Hotel. (11 x 14. c. 1890)

← ! probably late 60's or early 70's. – RLB

Mrs. Lee's parlor indicated that she was an eminent Victorian, much given to the style of her day. (8 x 10. 1869)

But it was as the Christian gentleman, who
salvaged true victory from seeming defeat,
that the South remembered him. (5 x 7. 1868)

PEOPLE

Michael Miley, photographed by his son
Henry during World War I. (5 x 7. 1915)

The young Miley, photographed by John Burdette in Staunton when Miley returned to civilian life. (3 x 4. 1866)

Miley posed his bride, the former Martha Mackey, just after their honeymoon. (3 x 4. 1871)

Mrs. Miley and the Miley boys. (5 x 8. c. 1910)

Michael Miley never lost his sense of the dramatic,
as this photograph of his son Henry—made when
Michael was in his seventies—shows. (8 x 10. c. 1916)

A nineteenth-century Washington and Lee Troubadour production of Shakespeare's *Hamlet*. The sad great Dane is at the extreme right. (11 x 14. c. 1898)

When Jefferson Davis visited Lee in Lexington, he posed for his Miley portrait. (4 x 5. 1868)

So did "Bigfoot" Wallace, who returned to his native Rockbridge County after a dramatic and legendary career in Texas. (4 x 6. c. 1885)

A Southern family portrait, with three generations included. (11 x 14. c. 1900)

Lexington's Mayor J. W. Houghawout was a confirmed
hunter who often startled the citizenry by sounding
his hunting horn on Main Street. (8 x 10. c. 1882)

College music at the turn of the century favored the banjo. In the back row, fourth from the right, is John W. Davis, the Democratic candidate for president in 1924. (8 x 10. 1892)

Girls from Lexington's Ann Smith Academy clustered around General "Stonewall" Jackson's grave for this picture. (6 x 8. x. 1870)

Matthew Fontaine Maury, "Pathfinder of the Seas," lying in state at the Virginia Military Institute. (9 x 12. 1873)

The 1901 V.M.I. football squad included George C. Marshall (x on jersey), Chief of Staff in World War II. (6 x 8. 1901)

The august members of a Negro lodge in Lexington pose for Miley in their Sunday best. (8 x 10. c. 1900)

The past seemed to reach out for Miley's lens when he posed Mrs. Jennie Crigler, Mrs. Mary Laird, Mrs. Mattie Hawes, and Mrs. John Laird for this picture. (8 x 10. c. 1905)

The well-dressed beau looked like this when he visited Miley. (8 x 10. 1892)

And the stylish belle (here Laura Rust) like this. (5 x 7. 1894)

54

One of the local farm boys invented the reaper
and made good. When Cyrus McCormick returned home, he sat for Miley. (8 x 10. 1878)

A Washington and Lee four-man crew working out on the Maury River. Rivalry between the two college crews (Harry Lee and Albert Sidney Johnston) dates from 1874. (8 x 10. 1891)

PLACES

"Forest Inn," a prosperous Valley hotel of the last century. (11 x 14. c. 1890)

A lock of the old James River and Kanawha Canal, with tow path and mule stable at the left. (5 x 7. c. 1874)

Miley never tired of photographing the quiet blue beauty of his valley. (6 x 8. 1874)

He considered this one of his best landscapes, and even gave it a name—"Volcano over House Mountain." (8 x 10. c. 1880)

To accent its size, Miley photographed Natural Bridge with three men on the footbridge, and two standing on top. (11 x 14. c. 1880)

The Tallyho coming in from Lynchburg. (8 x 10. c. 1878)

Lexington's Main Street on a Saturday afternoon. (7 x 9. c. 1890)

The blue beauty turned white in the winter snow. (7 x 9. 1877)

66

Everyday life in his little village provided much
material for Miley's camera. (11 x 14. c. 1875)

Starrett's Mill, near Timber Ridge, Virginia. (11 x 14. 1878)

"Thorn Hill," built in 1793, was an early example
of Greek Revival architecture and home of a Revolutionary soldier, John Bowyer. (8 x 10. c. 1875)

Nothing as bizarre as the log-cabin Gothic of the Armentrout
House on the road to Goshen escaped Miley. (7 x 9. 1883)

To live in Lexington is to look at mountains. (8 x 10. c. 1882)

When Miley went to visit and photograph his mountain friends, the girls got out their hats and the boys their rifles. (11 x 14. c. 1900)

71

V.M.I. was rebuilt after General Hunter's raid, and looked like this a quarter century later. The road in the foreground is now U.S. 11. (8 x 10. 1908)

APPENDICES

NOTE ON THE APPENDICES

THE MILEY COLLECTION, now in the possession of the Virginia Historical Society, is housed in the Virginia State Library, Richmond, Virginia. It consists of approximately 15,000 negatives in the following sizes: 100 of 4 x 3 inches; 7,400 of 7 x 5; 5,000 of 8 x 5; 2,000 of 10 x 8; 350 of 14 x 11; 100 of 20 x 17; and 50 of 24 x 20. About half of these were taken by Michael Miley between 1866 and 1910; the rest were made by Henry M. Miley, sometimes with the assistance of his father Michael. Extensive as the quantity of the collection is, few in America equalling it, it is even more impressive in its quality. Here are recorded not only the facts, but the spirit of two generations of American life as it was lived in the Shenandoah Valley.

The Rockefeller Foundation provided in 1940 the necessary funds to purchase the Miley Collection and move it from Lexington, Virginia, to Richmond, where it could be properly and safely stored. On April 20, 1940, Henry Mackey Miley transferred copyrights on material and photographs to the Virginia Historical Society, and the collection was moved in fifty-two specially constructed wooden boxes.

The Virginia State Chamber of Commerce undertook to have an inventory made and index files completed of the negatives.

The Writers' Project of the Works Progress Administration made available the services of Thomas Claiborne Carrington for this task. So important was his contribution to the Miley story, and so instrumental was his work as a background of this present study, that we must acknowledge Carrington's contribution.

Mr. Carrington was born in Halifax County, Virginia, on July 21, 1886; he left school in 1906 to work in the Escondidas de Coahuila mines in Mexico. After a hectic career in Mexico and various regions of the United States, he joined the Richmond group of the Works Progress Administration Virginia Writers' Project in 1937. When the Virginia Historical Society procured the Miley Collection, he was requested to identify and list the negatives. While he did not complete the job, nor reach any completely adequate way of classifying the diverse collection, he did manage to bring considerable order out of the chaos that he found when the boxes were unpacked. The task that confronted him in 1940 was quite staggering. Many of the invaluable Miley negatives, as Mr. Carrington pointed out in his November 30, 1940, report, were scratched and dirt-stained, and a number of the big plates were broken; fewer than 60 per cent were numbered or marked in any way. After the workers of the Writers' Project had cleaned all the negatives, Mr. Carrington began the long-overdue and arduous task of trying to identify the thousands of unmarked negatives. He visited Lexington with a number of prints made from unidentified negatives, where several gentlemen thoroughly familiar with local history, including Dr. Leslie Lyle Campbell, Dr. Edmund P. Tompkins, Col. William Couper, and Capt. Greenlee D. Letcher assisted so far as their knowledge allowed. Despite these and other similar efforts, the complete cataloging of the Miley Collection, which was abandoned when the Writers' Project was terminated, still remains to be done. There is small chance that some of the more obscure negatives will ever be identified.

This does not mean, of course, that most of the famous Mileys are not carefully marked, filed, and preserved. A complete record of all the Lee negatives, and all the experimental color negatives, exists, and is printed in part below. These groups are by all odds those of greatest national interest and concern. Less important, but still significant, is the list made by Michael Miley himself of his subjects from the establishment of his studio in 1866 through the first decade of the twentieth century. Although this is the most authoritative and important major catalog of Miley's works, it excludes a number of negatives which Miley apparently did not consider up to his standards and includes some that were lost in the disastrous fire of 1907. The corrected copy is now in the library of the Virginia Historical Society.

APPENDIX I

The Robert E. Lee Series of Negatives

THIS GROUP contains the most historical of all of Miley's negatives, and is divided into five sections: personal negatives, statues and memorials, buildings and personalia, letters and documents, and the Lee family. The negative numbers listed on the pages following are Miley's and have been preserved in this list, as have the size of the glass plates.

Unfortunately we do not have the dates of all the Miley portraits of Lee. The first cataloging was attempted by George Washington Custis Lee for the tenth volume of Miller's *Photographic History of the Civil War* (1912). Apparently no one else continued the work until T. C. Carrington's

day. At the moment, Robert Lilley of Mayfield Heights, Ohio, is engaged upon an intensive technical study of all the Lee photographs. The list following does not include all Miley pictures dealing with the Lees, but only those now owned by the Virginia Historical Society. Since all of them were on glass plates, some must certainly have been broken; and the additional hazards of the 1907 fire and the removal of the fragile collection to Richmond must also have taken its toll. Still the Lee lists which follow are of prime historical importance and show how thoroughly Miley went about putting the Lee story on glass for posterity.

THE ROBERT E. LEE SERIES OF NEGATIVES

SECTION ONE

Personal Negatives of Gen. R. E. Lee (1807-1870)

LISTED IN CHRONOLOGICAL ORDER

Nos. & Sizes

[280 to 287 inc.]
8 x 10
IN DRESS UNIFORM OF LIEUTENANT OF ENGINEERS, U. S. A. Made soon after his marriage, which occurred June 30, 1831. Copy of first painting made of Lee. These eight negatives were photographed in color.

[277-78-79]
5 x 7
Copy of the above painting, but not made in color. 11 Negatives

Nos. & Sizes

[O.S. 748]
5 x 8

IN CIVILIAN DRESS WITH ONE OF HIS SONS WHEN LATTER WAS CHILD. Only known copy of old daguerreotype, made for Lee's daughter.

[198]
5 x 7

IN DRESS UNIFORM OF CAPTAIN OF ENGINEERS, U.S.A. Copy of daguerreotype made about 1846, autographed by Lee. The original is in the Confederate Museum at Richmond.

[256, 258]
4 x 5

IN UNDRESS COAT OF COLONEL, U.S.A., AS SUPERINTEND-ENT, WEST POINT. Copy of painting made about 1855, probably by R. S. Weir, the professor of painting and drawing at West Point. 2 Negatives

[88]
5 x 7

IN UNIFORM OF GENERAL OF CONFEDERATE ARMY, STANDING. Made in 1862-63 when Lee's armies were victorious.

[90, 176, 190, 221]
5 x 7

IN UNIFORM OF GENERAL OF CONFEDERATE ARMY, BUST IN PROFILE. Made in 1863 at height of Lee's military career. 4 Negatives

[1, 8, 105, 57, 61, 111]
8 x 10
[175]
5 x 7

IN UNIFORM OF GENERAL OF CONFEDERATE ARMY, BUST IN PROFILE. Copies of painting made by the artist Pioto. Nos. 105, 111, and 175 were made in color. 7 Negatives

[138]
8 x 10

LAST MEETING OF GENERALS LEE AND JACKSON, ON HORSEBACK; IN BACKGROUND ARE COLS. WALTER H. TAYLOR AND CHARLES MARSHALL, AIDES TO LEE, AND COL. A. S. PENDLETON, AIDE TO JACKSON. Copy of an ideal likeness painted by Julio, now in the Cabildo of the Louisiana State Museum at New Orleans.

[275]
11 x 14
[9, 10, 51]
8 x 10
[86]
5 x 7

AS GENERAL, C. S. A., STANDING, WEARING SWORD AND SASH. Copy of an ideal likeness by Theodore Pine, painted in 1904. Original in Lee Chapel, Washington & Lee University. 5 Negatives

[13, 49, 50 and 52]
8 x 10
[84]
5 x 7

IN UNIFORM OF GENERAL, C. S. A., SEATED. FACE IN PRO-FILE. Copy of photograph made by Brady of Washington at 707 East Franklin Street, Richmond, home of Lee family during the war. Taken in 1865 while Lee was staying there for a short time after the surrender at Appomattox. 5 Negatives

78

The Robert E. Lee Negatives

[44, 261, 272, 273, 137]
5 x 7

IN UNIFORM OF GENERAL, C. S. A., TAKEN WITH HIS SON, GENERAL G. W. C. LEE. Copy of photograph by Brady of Washington after the surrender at Appomattox, at 707 East Franklin Street, Richmond, home of the Lee family during the war. 5 Negatives

[112]
5 x 7

SEATED WITH HIS SON, GEN. G. W. C. LEE, STANDING RIGHT, and COL. W. H. TAYLOR, HIS AIDE, STANDING LEFT. ALL IN UNIFORM. Copy of photograph by Brady of Washington made at 707 East Franklin Street, Richmond, after the surrender at Appomattox.

[303]
5 x 7

LEE, IN CENTER, WITH TWENTY OF HIS GENERALS. All busts, and all in civilian clothes.

[14, 56, 108]
8 x 10
[276]
11 x 14

LEE ON "TRAVELLER," HIS FAVORITE HORSE DURING AND AFTER THE WAR. Photo made at Lexington about 1866. 4 Negatives

[240]
5 x 7
[4]
8 x 10

IN CIVILIAN CLOTHES, HEAD AND SHOULDERS. Taken at Lexington, Va. about 1868, while Lee was President of Washington College. 2 Negatives

[115]
5 x 8

IN CIVILIAN CLOTHES, HEAD AND SHOULDERS. Taken in 1868 while President of Washington College, Lexington.

[87]
5 x 7
[158]
8 x 10

IN CIVILIAN CLOTHES, BUST. Taken in 1868 or 1869. Known as "The Smiling Picture of Lee." 2 Negatives

[O.S. 1532]
6½ x 8½

IN CIVILIAN CLOTHES, FULL LENGTH FIGURE, STANDING. Made in 1869 in the closing years of his life at Lexington.

[104]
8 x 10

IN CIVILIAN CLOTHES, HEAD AND SHOULDERS. One of the last photographs of Lee, made in 1869.

[20]
6½ x 8½

IN CIVILIAN CLOTHES. THE HEAD, WITH HAIR AND BEARD ENTIRELY WHITE. The last picture made of Lee; taken at Lexington a few months before his death. Called "The Saddest Face in History."

[289]
11 x 14
[290]
5 x 8

LEE'S BODY AS IT LAY IN STATE IN THE CHAPEL OF WASHINGTON COLLEGE FROM THE AFTERNOON OF FRIDAY,

OCT. 14th, 1870, TO NOON ON SATURDAY, OCT. 15th, GUARDED BY STUDENTS OF WASHINGTON COLLEGE. 2 Negatives

[300]
11 X 14

FUNERAL OF LEE, OCTOBER 15, 1870; SHOWING THE CROWDS OUTSIDE THE CHAPEL AND ON THE CAMPUS OF WASHINGTON COLLEGE, LEXINGTON.

[303]
8 X 10

OBITUARY OF LEE PUBLISHED OCTOBER 12th, 1870, IN THE VIRGINIA GAZETTE OF LEXINGTON, VA.

THE ROBERT E. LEE SERIES OF NEGATIVES

SECTION TWO

Statues and Memorials

[369 to 376 inc., 294-95-96]
11 X 14

THE RECUMBENT STATUE OF LEE BY E. V. VALENTINE IN LEE CHAPEL, WASHINGTON & LEE UNIVERSITY, LEXINGTON, VA. Valentine took measurements and modeled a bust used for this work when Lee was President of Washington College. Figure, full length on its base, in rear of rostrum of chapel.

[2, 55]
8 X 10

Figure, full length on its base, in rear of rostrum of chapel.

[74, 298]
5 X 8

Figure, full length on its base, in rear of rostrum of chapel.

[297]
11 X 14

Figure, half length on its base, in rear of rostrum of chapel.

[291, 292]
17 X 20

Figure, full length showing view of interior of chapel.

[293]
11 X 14

Figure, full length showing view of interior of chapel.

[6, 53]
8 X 10

Figure, full length showing view of interior of chapel.

[218]
8 X 10

Seen through scrolled iron gates, Confederate flags on each side.

[241]
8 X 10

Seen with iron gates open and Confederate flags on each side.

Nos. & Sizes

[299]
8 x 10

Seen with Confederate flags before closed gates. 24 Negatives
These are battle flags, scarred with many bullet holes.

[384]
11 x 14

MODEL OF A. FRED VOLCK'S STATUETTE OF LEE.
In Museum of the Virginia Military Institute, Lexington.

[67]
5 x 7

LEE CHAPEL, EXTERIOR, WASHINGTON & LEE UNIVERSITY.

[98, 99]
8 x 10

ROBERT E. LEE MEMORIAL CHURCH (EPISCOPAL), LEXING-
TON, VA.

[68]
5 x 7

ROBERT E. LEE MEMORIAL CHURCH (EPISCOPAL), LEXING-
TON, VA.

[385]
11 x 14

ROBERT E. LEE MEMORIAL CHURCH (EPISCOPAL), LEXING-
TON, VA.

[479]
17 x 20

ROBERT E. LEE MEMORIAL CHURCH (EPISCOPAL), LEXING-
TON, VA. 5 Negatives

THE ROBERT E. LEE SERIES OF NEGATIVES

SECTION THREE

Homes, Office and Personalia

[306]
8 x 10

STRATFORD, WESTMORELAND COUNTY, VA., ANCESTRAL
HOME OF THE LEE FAMILY, BUILT BY THOMAS LEE ABOUT
1729.   Gen. Lee lived here until he was four, the family then moving to
Alexandria. Since 1929, Stratford has been owned by the Robert E. Lee
Memorial Foundation. Copy of original picture owned by G. W. C. Lee.

[307]
8 x 10

ARLINGTON, LEE'S HOME FROM HIS MARRIAGE TO MARY
CUSTIS IN 1831, UNTIL HE JOINED THE CONFEDERACY IN
1861, WHEN THE FAMILY WAS EXPELLED. The property was
confiscated by the Federal government for non-payment of taxes. Building of Arlington was begun in 1802 by G. W. P. Custis, grandson of
Martha Washington and father-in-law of Gen. Lee. The grounds are now
a national cemetery and the house is a museum.

Nos. & Sizes

[119, 307, 308, 309]
8 x 10

LEE'S FIRST HOME IN LEXINGTON, CALLED "OLD" PRESI-DENT'S HOUSE. He lived here from Dec. 2, 1865 to June 1869. Carpets and hangings for the house formerly were used at Arlington; the Custis and Washington portraits, preserved by relatives, also now were reclaimed. The family silver, buried during the fighting, was dug up and restored to use. Furniture for Mrs. Lee's room, supplied by the ladies of Lexington, was designed by the author, Margaret Preston. This house formerly was the home of Doctor George Junkin, President of Washington College, 1848-1861; his daughter, Elinor, was the first wife of Stonewall Jackson, who also lived here for a time. 4 Negatives

[92, 235-36, 310, 311]
8 x 10
[312]
5 x 8

LEE'S SECOND HOME IN LEXINGTON. Lee died in this house, Oct. 12, 1870. The family lived here from June 1869, until some time after Lee's death. Later it was occupied by G. W. C. Lee. 6 Negatives

[314]
8 x 10

INTERIOR OF LEE'S SECOND HOME IN LEXINGTON. On the walls are portraits of the Lee and Custis families.

[377, 313]
8 x 10

PIANO USED IN BOTH LEXINGTON HOMES. Presented to Gen. Lee by the maker, Stieff, of Baltimore. 2 Negatives

[250, 251]
8 x 10
[254, 315]
5 x 7

OFFICE IN WASHINGTON COLLEGE, AS LEE LEFT IT FOR THE LAST TIME ON SEPT. 28, 1870. His last act in this room was to grant a student's request to autograph a picture of himself. 4 Negatives

[316]
8 x 10

TRAVELING TRUNK, WITH EATING UTENSILS USED IN THE WAR. DR. HENRY L. SMITH, PRESIDENT OF WASHING-TON & LEE, IS SHOWN HOLDING A CUP. When the unearthed silver of the Lee family was found too tarnished for use at the family's first meal in Lexington, the cutlery from this trunk was utilized.

[317]
5 x 7

MESS KIT USED DURING WAR BETWEEN THE STATES.

[318]
8 x 10

UNVEILING OF TABLET TO LEE'S HORSE IN WAR AND PEACE, "TRAVELLER."

The Robert E. Lee Negatives

THE ROBERT E. LEE SERIES OF NEGATIVES

SECTION FOUR

Letters and Documents

Nos. & Sizes

[328]
8 x 10

SCHEDULE OF PROPERTY COMPOSING HIS ESTATE AT-
TACHED TO THE PRECEDING WILL OF LEE. In this document he
states his desire that a Negro slave and her children at White House, New
Kent County, Va., be liberated as soon as possible. These were the only
slaves owned by Lee personally.

THE ROBERT E. LEE SERIES OF NEGATIVES

SECTION FIVE

The Lee Family

[329]
11 x 14

RICHARD LEE, DIED 1664, FIRST OF THE FAMILY IN AMERICA.
Copy of painting by an unknown artist. Came to Colony of Virginia in
1640. Was Attorney General and Member of the King's Council.

[255]
5 x 8
[194, 330-1-2]
8 x 10
[333-4-5]
11 x 14

GEN. HENRY LEE, KNOWN AS LIGHT HORSE HARRY, 1756-
1818, FATHER OF ROBERT E. LEE. Was General in Revolutionary
War; Governor of Virginia, 1791-1794. Copy of painting by Gilbert
Stuart. 8 Negatives. Seven of these negatives were made in color.

[336-7-8, 339-
340, 341-342]
8 x 10

MRS. ROBERT E. LEE, 1808-1873, BORN MARY ANN RANDOLPH
CUSTIS. Copy of painting, by unknown artist, made after marriage
about 1831. These seven negatives were all made in color.

[343]
5 x 7

Copy of painting, by unknown artist, made after marriage, about 1831.

[18]
6 x 8

Copy of photograph made in 1858 at Arlington.

[344]
3 x 4

Seated in wheel-chair. Made at Lexington, Va., about 1866.

[128]
5 x 8

Seated in wheel-chair. Made at Lexington in old age.

[381]
16 x 20

Seated in wheel-chair. Made at Lexington in old age.

[124]
5 x 8

Made at Lexington shortly before her death. 13 Negatives

The Robert E. Lee Negatives

[36-222]
5 x 7

GEORGE WASHINGTON CUSTIS LEE, 1832-1913, GENERAL ROBERT E. LEE'S ELDEST SON. Copy of photograph made when cadet at West Point. Was Major-General, C. S. A., Instructor at V. M. I., 1865-1870; President of Washington & Lee University, 1870-1897.

[345-46, 113, 347]
5 x 7
[382]
17 x 20

As President of Washington & Lee University. Made about 1880. 7 Negatives

[371]
5 x 8

Made at Lexington in 1870.

[238]
8½ x 6

WILLIAM HENRY FITZHUGH LEE, 1837-1891, GEN. LEE'S SECOND SON. Copy of portrait as young man in uniform. Major General U. S. A.

[31-32]
5 x 8

Made in middle age.

[241-5004]
5 x 8

Made in old age, 1888.

[369]
11 x 14

Made in old age. 6 Negatives

[O.S. 719]
5 x 8

CAPTAIN ROBERT E. LEE, JR., 1843-1914, GEN. LEE'S YOUNGEST SON. Made about 1881. Was Private and later a Captain in C. S. A.

[223-245]
5 x 7

Made in middle age, between 1886-1892.

[348]
5 x 7

Made in 1907 at the age of 64. 4 Negatives

[349]
5 x 8

THE THREE SONS OF GENERAL LEE. G. W. C. Lee, Standing; W. H. F. Lee and R. E. Lee, Jr., Seated. Made in 1888.

[O.S. 747]
5 x 8
[350-51]
3 x 4

MARY CUSTIS LEE, OLDEST DAUGHTER OF GEN. LEE, 1835-1918. 3 Negatives

[O.S. 1531]
6½ x 8½

ELEANOR AGNES LEE, THIRD DAUGHTER OF GEN. LEE, 1842-1873.

[352]
3 x 4

MILDRED CHILDE LEE, YOUNGEST DAUGHTER OF GEN. LEE, 1846-1905.

Nos. & Sizes

NO PICTURE IS KNOWN EVER TO HAVE BEEN TAKEN OF
ANNE CARTER, GEN. LEE'S SECOND DAUGHTER.

[O.S. 2654[
5 x 8

GEORGE BOLLING LEE, BORN 1872, SON OF W. H. F. LEE,
GRANDSON OF GEN. LEE. Trustee of Washington and Lee University; Physician in New York City.

[353-54]
5 x 7

ANNE CARTER AND MARY CUSTIS LEE, CHILDREN OF R. E.
LEE, JR.

[O.S. 2653]
5 x 8

ROBERT E. LEE, 3rd. SON OF W. H. F. LEE, GRANDSON OF
GEN. LEE, 1869-1922. Trustee of Washington & Lee University.

[368]
8 x 10

GEORGE WASHINGTON PARKE CUSTIS, 1781-1857, FATHER
OF MRS. R. E. LEE, SON OF JOHN PARKE CUSTIS, GRANDSON
OF MRS. GEO. WASHINGTON. Ward of George Washington and
reared at Mt. Vernon. 4 Negatives
In old age. Copy of painting by Wollaston.

[378]
5 x 8

As a youth. Copy of painting supposedly by Stearnes.

[379]
5 x 8

As a youth. Copy of miniature by unknown artist.

[380]
5 x 8

As young man, in uniform of an aide-de-camp. Copy, unknown artist.

[355]
5 x 8

MRS. G. W. P. CUSTIS, 1788-1852, MOTHER OF MRS. R. E. LEE.
Born Mary Lee Fitzhugh. 2 Negatives
Copy of portrait made when a young woman.

[356]
5 x 8

Made in middle age. Copy of old photograph.

[357-8-9]
5 x 8

GENERAL FITZHUGH LEE, 1835-1905, NEPHEW OF GEN. R. E.
LEE. Major General in War Between the States and in Spanish-American
War; Governor of Virginia, 1886-1889. 3 Negatives

[360]
17 x 20

ELLEN LEE, BORN 1873, DAUGHTER OF GENERAL FITZHUGH
LEE. Wife of Capt. James Rhea, U. S. A.

The Robert E. Lee Negatives

[362]
5 x 8

LETTER OF G. W. C. LEE DATED AUGUST, 1894, TESTIFYING THAT A CERTAIN ENGRAVING IS OF AN OIL PAINTING OF MRS. GEORGE WASHINGTON.

[363]
8 x 8

LETTER OF G. W. C. LEE TESTIFYING THAT A CERTAIN PHOTOGRAPH IS OF AN OIL PAINTING OF MRS. GEORGE WASHINGTON.

[366]
8 x 10

COPY OF PAINTING OF UNKNOWN MAN BY VAN DYKE, IN LEE CHAPEL.

[367]
8 x 10

COPY OF PAINTING OF UNKNOWN WOMAN BY VAN DYKE, IN LEE CHAPEL. Originals of both the above paintings were owned by G. W. C. Lee. 2 Negatives

[364]
5 x 7

COAT OF ARMS OF THE LEE FAMILY. 2 Negatives

[365]
6½ x 8½

COAT OF ARMS OF THE LEE FAMILY.

[131]
8 x 10

GENEALOGICAL TREE OF THE LEE FAMILY, STARTING WITH RICHARD LEE.

[361]
8 x 10

TABLETS IN LEE CHAPEL ABOVE THE TOMBS OF THE LEE FAMILY WHO ARE BURIED IN THE CRYPT BELOW. They include Gen. R. E. Lee, Mrs. Mary Custis Lee, their children, Mary Custis, Eleanor Agnes, Mildred Childe and George Washington Custis; also Gen. Henry Lee, father of Robert E. Lee.

APPENDIX II

The Miley Collection of Historical, Photographic Negatives

The Miley Negatives Made in Color

Sizes

8 x 10   8 Negatives. Gen. R. E. Lee, As Lieutenant, U. S. A., 1831.
Copy of painting made by Benj. West.

[1]
5 x 7
[2]
8 x 10   3 Negatives. Gen. R. E. Lee, As General, C. S. A., 1863.
Copy of painting made by Pioto.

8 x 10   7 Negatives. Mrs. R. E. Lee, about 1831.
Copy of painting by an unknown artist.

[3]
11 x 14
[4]
8 x 10   7 Negatives. Gen. Henry Lee, as General in Continental Army.
Copy of painting by Gilbert Stuart.

8 x 10   7 Negatives. Gen. T. J. Jackson, in 1862.
Copy of photograph made at Winchester, Va.

[9]
11 x 14
[9]
8 x 10   18 Negatives. George Washington, As Colonel of Virginia Militia.
Copy of painting by Chas. Willson Peale.

8 x 10   10 Negatives. George Washington, in old age.
Copy of painting made by Sharples.

11 x 14   3 Negatives. Mrs. Martha Dandridge Custis, in 1757.
Copy of painting by John Wollaston.

8 x 10   7 Negatives. Mrs. George Washington, (?). Artist not known.
This negative is labeled by Michael Miley, "Mrs. Geo. Washington."

[3]
11 x 14
[6]
8 x 10   9 Negatives. Eleanor Parke Custis, as young woman.
Copy of painting by Gilbert Stuart.

88

Negatives Made in Color

[3]
11 X 14
[3]
8 x 10

6 Negatives. John Parke Custis and Martha Parke Custis, as children. Grandchildren of Mrs. George Washington.

Copy of painting by John Wollaston.

[4]
11 X 14
[5]
8 x 10

9 Negatives. Col. Daniel Parke. In uniform of British Officer.

Copy of painting by Godfrey Kneller.

8 x 10

7 Negatives. Mrs. John Custis, daughter of Col. Daniel Parke.

[4]
8 x 10
[10]
5 X 7

14 Negatives. Mrs. Virginia Moore. Used as model; original photograph.

8 x 10

3 Negatives. Miss Jennie Hopkins. Original photograph.

8 x 10

8 Negatives. The Virginia Military Institute, about 1896.

Original photograph.

17 X 14

3 Negatives. The Battle of New Market.

Copy of painting by B. W. Clinedinst.

8 x 10

7 Negatives. The Juniata River. Copy of painting.

8 x 10

5 Negatives. Hay Making. Copy of painting by James Burkett.

[6]
8 x 10
[7]
5 X 7

13 Negatives. Of Flowers.

8 x 10

16 Negatives. Of Fruit. Peaches.

APPENDIX III

United States Patent Office.

*Michael Miley and Henry Mackey Miley, of Lexington, Virginia,
Assignors to Miley Colour Photograph Company,
of New York, N. Y.*

COLOR PHOTOGRAPH AND ART OF MAKING SAME.

SPECIFICATION forming part of Letters Patent No. 711,875, dated October 21, 1902.
Application filed March 31, 1902. Serial No. 100,824. (No specimens.)

To all whom it may concern:

Be it known that we, MICHAEL MILEY and HENRY MACKEY MILEY, citizens of the United States, and residents of Lexington, in the county of Rockbridge and State of Virginia, have invented a new and useful Improvement in Color Photographs, of which the following is a specification.

Our invention relates to color photography; and it consists in the product and process hereinafter described.

In carrying out our process we proceed as follows: Negatives are made by the tricolor process, using three sensitized plates and three screens, the screens being red, green, and violet, respectively, and the coloring-matter of each screen being placed between thin glass. Such screens can be procured from photographic-supply houses. These screens are manufactured with the greatest care, with the idea of representing as near as possible the primary-color areas of the photographed object. Care should be

taken to select only those screens which have been tested for color value and guaranteed.

With the red screen an orthochromatic plate flowed with a cyanin solution is used. With the green screen an orthochromatic plate is used, and with the violet screen a plain gelatino-silver-bromid plate is used. Detailed explanation of this step is unnecessary, inasmuch as the photographic-supply houses which furnish the color screens furnish also full directions in regard to the preparation of plates used in connection therewith and time of exposure. After exposure, the plates being developed, we have three negatives—one through the red screen, one through the green screen, and one through the violet screen—varying in density in the different areas substantially in

The fall foliage on the Virginia Military Institute roadway was a challenge to his new color process. (c. 1908)

accordance with the color values of the three primary colors in the corresponding areas of the picture taken. From these negatives, taken successively through the red, green, and violet screens prints are made by the use of bichromated gelatin-pigment paper, (carbon tissue.) Inasmuch as it is our purpose and requisite to the end we have in view—to represent the primary colors of the object photographed—great care should be exercised in selecting pigments to take only those which when tested by spectrum give a color value closely approximating the spectrum of the color —red, blue, or yellow—they represent. A pigment having ninety per cent, or even somewhat less, of the spectrum value of its primary color can be used with good results. The nearer its color value approaches the spectrum of its primary color the better. The pigment thus stands in the picture as the effective representative of its primary color in the photographed object. Another controlling consideration in the selection of the pigments is that only those should be taken that are inert as regards gelatin in the sense that they do not affect the solubility of the latter, because the object we have in view is dependent upon the relative solubility of different areas of the gelatin-pigment paper, and a pigment which in itself would tend to render the gelatin insoluble or less soluble throughout the whole area of the paper would defeat that object. By employing, however, what we have termed an "inert pigment" the solubility of the gelatin remains unaffected, and consequently the pigment color in the picture will substantially conform to the area of its primary color in the photographed object. The pigment red, pigment yellow, and pigment blue are finally ground and embedded and thoroughly mixed with soluble gelatin coated on paper and dried. These papers can be prepared and made to order in the roll by carbon-tissue manufacturers, careful attention, as before said, being given to the pigments employed.

The paper when required for use can be sensitized in a bath of about five-per-cent solution of potassium bichromate for three minutes and dried in a dark room. The action of light in the coating thus sensitized is to render insoluble in hot water so much of the gelatin as is affected by the rays. The paper as thus prepared is ready for printing. The density of the three negatives is ascertained in any well-known way.

Using the red-screen negative we print the blue-pigment paper. From the green-screen negative the red-pigment paper is printed, and from the violet-screen negative the yellow-pigment paper is printed. We have now three gelatin-pigment papers the gelatin of which varies in solubility in the different pigment areas according to the color values in the corresponding areas of the respective three negatives just mentioned.

The development of the gelatin-pigment papers is in the following order:

Development of the red pigment.—A temporary support, generally a film of opaque flexible celluloid or, if preferable, glass or porcelain, is flowed with wax on one surface, and when the wax has set collodion is flowed over the wax. For the wax solution we prefer to use rosin, four drams, and beeswax, one dram, dissolved in turpentine, sixteen ounces. The collodion solution consists, preferably, of ether, eight ounces, alcohol, twelve ounces, and gun-cotton, one hundred grains. The absolute qualities of course may vary; but the proportions above stated will be found suitable for the purpose. When the collodion sets, but before it dries, the celluloid film is placed in cold water until it is required for use, the object being to maintain the collodion in adhesive condition. The red-pigment paper is soaked in cold water (58° Fahrenheit) until it becomes limp and is then squeegeed on the prepared surface of the celluloid and kept under pressure for about twenty minutes. The celluloid film and pigment-paper are then subjected to a hot-water bath at a temperature of about 100° Fahrenheit until the soluble gelatin by the action of the hot water begins to swell around the edges and exudes from between the celluloid and the paper. Beginning at one corner the paper is now stripped from the celluloid, carrying with it most of the still soluble gelatin and its contained pigment and leaving on the celluloid the light-struck gelatin, with its embedded pigments, as well as some soluble gelatin. By gentle agitation the free gelatin, together with so much pigment as it contains, is washed away. The remaining pigment accords substantially with the primary red color in the different portions of the photographed object. The insoluble gelatin, with its contained pigments, is now transferred to a piece of gelatin-coated paper, which forms the final support upon which the red, yellow, and blue pigment films are superposed, preferably in the order named. The gelatin transfer-paper is first put in cold water until it becomes limp and is then put in water having a temperature

of about 70° Fahrenheit until the gelatin begins to soften. It is then taken out of the bath and applied to and pressed upon the pigment-bearing surface of the celluloid and hung up to dry. The effect of the drying is that the paper frees itself from the celluloid by contraction of the gelatin, stripping the celluloid of its prepared surface, which remains on the transfer-paper. It is most important to get rid of the wax on the surface of the pigmented gelatin now on the transfer-paper in order to insure the complete and permanent adhesion of the pigment films when superposed, as will shortly be described. The wax cannot be effectively dissolved and removed by means of alcohol, ether, benzin, or the like; but by the application and use of collodion in the manner herein before specified this result can be obtained. When the transfer-paper is removed from the celluloid, we have the wax on the outermost surface of the paper, the collodion film next, and then the gelatin with its contained pigment. Now by rubbing the surface of the paper with a wash composed of equal parts of ether and alcohol the collodion is readily dissolved and removed and carries with it the wax on its surface, leaving a clean pigmented-gelatin surface.

Development of the yellow and blue pigments.—The development of the yellow pigment is effected in the same way, using, however, a transparent support, preferably flexible, such as transparent flexible celluloid. After development of the yellow pigment on the transparent support the latter is laid pigment-face downward upon the red-pigment face of the transparent paper, the red-pigment surface being first flowed

forming to the area of one of the primary colors of the photographed object, and directly superimposing said pictures, substantially as set forth.

3. The process of color photography which consists in printing from negatives by direct contact upon sensitized-pigment papers images of the primary-color areas of the same photographed object, and then directly superimposing said pigments, substantially as described.

4. The process of accurate color photography which consists in making separate pigment photographs of the same object on bichromated gelatin tissue containing inert red, yellow and blue pigments respectively, each having a color value substantially that of the primary color which it represents,

and directly superimposing said pigments, substantially as described.

5. The method of facilitating the removal of the wax from the face of the pigmented gelatin film, which consists in interposing a layer of collodion between the face of the film and the wax on the surface of the temporary support to which the said film is applied during the process of development, substantially as and for the purposes hereinbefore set forth.

In testimony whereof we have hereunto set our hands this 28th day of March, 1902.

MICHAEL MILEY.

HENRY MACKEY MILEY.

Witnesses:

J. W. MOORE,

ED. T. ROBINSON.

with a gelatin solution containing a few drops of a hardening agent, such as chrome-alum—say in the proportion of ten drops of saturated solution of chrome-alum to eight ounces water and one dram gelatin. After a proper coincidence of the color areas is established (this can be determined by observation through the transparent celluloid film) a slight pressure is brought to bear and the product is hung up to dry. The drying operation separates the celluloid film from the paper, as before described, and the surface of the latter being freed from collodion and wax we now have the paper bearing two superposed primary colors—red and yellow—of the photographed object. We proceed with the development and transfer of the blue pigment in the same way as with the yellow, except that as this is the final superposed film it is only necessary to wax the surface of the transparent celluloid film or other transparent support, omitting the collodion. The transfer-paper (the final support) will now bear the superposed pigments of the three primary colors—red, yellow, blue—in the order named, constituting a perfect color picture containing a very exact reproduction of the colors of the original object.

We prefer to superpose the pigments in the order stated, although, if desired, the red may be superposed on the yellow instead of the yellow on the red; but we find that to obtain the best results it is always desirable to superpose the blue last of all.

The accompanying drawings, which depict in the finished picture a young girl wearing a red dress, a blue sash, and a yellow hat, is a diagrammatic representation of the simplest expression of the invention, and even in this it is not possible to represent the combinations of pigments to which shadings and graduations of color are due.

Figure 1 represents at R a face view of the red-pigmented film with the red-color area appropriately lined thereon, and at *r* an edge view of said film on its temporary support. Fig. 2 represents at Y a face view of the yellow-pigmented film with the yellow-color area appropriately hatched thereon, and at *y* an edge view of said film on its temporary support. Fig. 3 represents at B the blue-pigmented film with the blue-color area appropriately lined thereon, and *b* is an edge view of the blue film on its temporary support. Fig. 4 is a face view representing the effect produced by the superimposition of the three films having the color areas R Y B depicted in the preceding figures, and at *b y r* is represented an edge view of the three films superimposed on their permanent support.

Having described our invention and the best way now known to us of carrying the same into practical effect, what we claim herein as new and of our own invention is as follows:

1. A color photograph consisting of directly superimposed inert primary-color pigments, having substantially the same color value as, and representing and conforming to the areas of, their respective primary colors in the photographed object, substantially as set forth.

2. The process of producing accurate color photographs which consists in making pigment pictures in inert primary colors each substantially representing and con-